Hold Sway

Also by Sally Ball

Wreck Me
Annus Mirabilis

Artist's Book

HOLD, with Jan Vičar

Hold Sway

Sally Ball

Barrow Street Press
New York City

Cover art from the cycle "HOLD": *La vague*, by Jan Vičar.
PVC relief, 200 x 250 cm, 2017. By permission of the artist.
Designed by Michelle Caraccia

Published 2019 by Barrow Street, Inc.
(501) (c) (3) corporation. All contributions are tax deductible.
Distributed by:
    Barrow Street Books
    P.O. Box 1558
    Kingston, RI 02881

Barrow Street Books are also distributed by Small Press Distribution,
SPD, 1341 Seventh Street, Berkeley, CA 94710-1409, spd@spdbooks.
org; (510) 524-1668, (800) 869-7553 (Toll-free within the US); amazon.
com; Ingram Periodicals Inc., 1240 Heil Quaker Blvd, PO Box 7000,
La Vergne, TN 37086-700 (615) 213-3574; and Armadillo & Co.,
7310 S. La Cienega Blvd, Inglewood, CA 90302, (310) 693-6061.

Special thanks to the University of Rhode Island English Department and
especially the PhD Program in English, 60 Upper College Road, Swan
114, Kingston, RI 02881, (401) 874-5931, which provide valuable
in-kind support, including graduate and undergraduate interns.

First Edition

Library of Congress Control Number: 2018968182

ISBN 978-0-9973184-7-0

for Martha and Ryan

CONTENTS

III.

Notes

Acknowledgments

"... certainty was still alive, the grass didn't fear anything yet. Soon you were going to call, my steps were going to join yours in the living sand."

—Greta Knutson

I.

Armistice Day

Now comes the moment before darkness
when the river is the sky's purple mirror

and the riverbank goes dark, the bridge goes dark, everything
melts into nothing save the light that faces itself.
As if it had come to an understanding, as if

it were listening to logic—
then very soon,
there's nothing to see.

Invitation If I Can Remember How

I said in the galvanized bucket of my skull
What is fear? because I thrummed
with it and wanted not to, and then
this rustle: a quick flock of gray and white
erupted beneath the window,
and whooshed out, crossing the river.

A car passed on the bridge. All the wing-sounds
and wheel-sounds rattled in the bucket.
Along with the last leaves straining from the trees.

My heart took ten seconds of joy
from the ascendant birds and then
pulsed its caffeinated uh-uh.

As if I were not a bucket but a wire
or a river, coursing.
In that apparently inexhaustible way.

I am a bucket. Fill me up?

I am the kind of metal thing you hate to touch
because the clang is unpleasant to the ear. Always a scrape
against no-matter-the-grit.

Maybe you can use water from the river.

Maybe you can plunge your face in,

open your eyes.

Or maybe I'm the river after all.
Coursing,

a body that unfurls even as it's held.
Which lasts, this current, this ongoing,

maybe it lasts.

Temple Example

The mind doesn't do what we want it to do.

Mine plays speed Scrabble; it sifts pages and pages

of pictures of shoes. Palmyra goodbye. Temple of Bel not a pun

but a ruin. A ruined ruin, a ruin sent to oblivion

on purpose. Who cares if I fold up at my desk

a heap of angry sorrow. Not any candidate,

no ambassador. Sign a petition, email some senators—

I make nothing happen. I make

nothing but orders, seven-letter words, coffee

with the hard water from the oleander-pierced pipes

with their roaches and mud. A temple

stood for twenty centuries and today *The New York Times*

shows us its new life as dust. *Baal* is how they spell it.

A neat aerial square of nothing now. The world wants

what from us in reply to the hatred of the mind?

I should say "soul," I know, or "history" or "culture,"

but probably only the mind can thwart destructions.

In America, the mind is also hated,

by whosoever sells us shoes and phones. We are subtle

here, give lots of money to the arts.

Leave No Trace

The boy went hiking for a month

He took his books

boots from Italy meant for Alps and weather

and with his friends 400 pounds

of food: lentils lentils lentils

quinoa! lentils

He left Coetzee's *Disgrace*

on a rock in the sun and hiked on

and then remembered two miles out

                         so two went back

He said they searched in case

the spot was misremembered

but the book was gone   two miles

to rejoin the resting others

Four extra miles that day

Three chapters in and so much

left to find out   Everyone rolling

their eyes   Poor boy

poor ruffled book flickering in the wind

and then a swoop   pages as mild drag

against this mama hawk   swoop

swoop and then she's busy shredding

when her mate returns   stalks

or pine needles   husks   in his beak

homemaking   rough twiggy nest

as big as a small wheelbarrow

Softened now   the strips of pages

weathered and jostled and rumpled

and macerated (sort of) (beakily)

and in those pages   tucked and warm

two or three blue eggs

two or three speckled chests

and those bleating cries

How Do You Do It

Was the abusive coach actually
                     a menace or
just bad timing, his offhand
                         remark that fell
into a loop of self-loathing,
                         adding an "outside voice"
on top of the inside one,
                         (which can at least be doubted, right?
since it comes from the stupid self—). My girl.

Stupid self—everyone valuable
                         so sui-accuses,
part of being sentient
                         and not evil
is that self-consciousness, -distrust,
                         now and then.
Excoriations under a rock. Grief rock.

Our one girl. Alongside two brothers
                         and the normal of now:
college apps, thank-you notes,
                         first responder
certification. (Do I worry
                         about him, or
about what he'll see?) Homework
                         and *Self Care:*
exercise and good books, coffee
                         and solitude or new friends
or none, none today, and how much
                         competition

makes sense if you don't
                 homeschool and don't play
(tennis) six hours a day six days a week . . .
                 How often,
how little, how hard, how soon—

Each one with a spiraling list,
                 small woes, big ones,
I'm here and I'm ready but also
                 spent the afternoon learning
(from church ladies) how to keep kids safe
                 from *Sexual Predators*—
"talented, resourceful, authoritative."

Like the security guard who bought Cokes
                 offered rides, gave money,
suggested paintball (a team)
                 Don't tell your parents. . . .
Two boys, my oldest and his friend.
                 The friend said Let's not tell.
The double betrayal
                 it then was to tell us.
When the police went to question
                 the guard, he had emptied
his apartment and fled. *Pffst.*
                 Which means it was real.
Fucking real. Only one boy

able, willing, to tell. And me,
                dumb luck
to get between my kids and the threats,
                or not to get there.
To mean well but be weak
                or too late. We have work,
we make dinner or
                time or haste. Or we don't.
We don't make it. When will that be?

Furious Deities

(Plate 40   Bardo Mural   Ladakh, India)

Two goats devour a man with an erect cock
and open eyes. The other scenes
are harder to discern: the horse
will trample the man beneath him,
or is it rape? The man looks bored.
And what seems like mild concern
mottles the third man's wrinkled face—
he's the captive of another goat.
The porn, apparently, derives from a tragedy
of appetite. The lesson has to do with poise
and how it leads to liberation. Everyone's well-groomed:
the goats and horses wear regalia, their fur
curls neatly, their only wildness in the vicious kicking legs
and ass-delecting tongues, the men have neat
short hair and otherwise are nude.
They are, in any case, the prey.
And unperturbed. They are all men.
And dipping in—as if to join? or for a better look?—
two passing cranes, one with an eyeball
dangling from its beak. That eye unsocketed, and then
some flower-fronds. Cranes: those birds
sing and dance. They mate for life.

Sight Management

["*Hyperspace Bypass Construction Zone* is an art installation, a series of large-scale polyhedrons that investigates geometry through light and shadow. . . . They are lit from the inside and cast intricate, colorful shadows all around." —Yelena Filipchuk & Serge Beaulieu]

Chapter 1. Hyperspace Bypass

Beyond light speed, i.e. imaginary,
because we want to outwit nature,
all the *knowns*—

as if we knew. Every avant turns
into a cliché in time.

Ha! In "time":

the *bypass* is a hedge, right? We're doing hyperspace
in a new way, it has an access road,

a clover leaf.

Chapter 2. Luck

To break a law of nature,
you'll need either
Dick Blick
or a metaphor.

Chapter 3. Construction Zone

… where work's ongoing,
where something's being made right now,
in progress.

Here, brass boxes blaze with static polygons,
cages whose only "prisoner" is light:
light gets away. Keats' grave

says *Here lies one whose name was writ in water.*

The brass boxes say *Everything we make
cannot be held. Everything we care about.
It spills.* They gleam at 4 p.m. and vanish
after dark, you find them then by what pours out.

Yesterday I had a cocktail named to honor Robert Frost,
a *Nothing Gold Can Stay.* The glass that held it

was a globe, a bulb, diffusing
golden light that disappeared with every sip—

Chapter 4: 40 Light Years

away we found some planets
that might have oceans, life.

Found them how? Their dwarf star—
around which they orbit as we orbit the sun—
would dim from time to time: remote eclipses!

We found these possibly hospitable alternate homes
because they interrupted our view of dwarfstarlight.

We were looking at something we stopped
being able to see
and thus discerned a different presence. Presences.

It isn't only billionaires who'll want to go—

Jeff & Elon.

Let's write our names in water and in ink.
Then name those seven planets,
draw them in oils, acrylics, watercolor.
Model them in brass.

Their dwarf sun's name is Trappist-1,
acronymish for TRAnsiting
                    Planets and
                    PlanetesImals
                    Small
                    Telescope

Not a trap or cage, that mini-star, not a monk
who microbrews. A way of looking that depends

on noticing what we no longer see.

What to Do with Dead Birds

(Plate 36   Birds' Heads   Ladakh, India)

Sew the falcon's head to a coin.
Use twine, thread it through his nostril,
and use the coin shaped like a washer—or use a washer.

Let there be feathers but no eyes,
and sever the head from the body.
You only need to keep
the very head, no neck, no wings.

If you tether it with twine
it's easier to hold and hang, more talismanic.

What are they for?
—the duck and flycatchers, beaks larger than their brains,
the hooked pincer of the falcon?

You never know.

Even if you think you know,
chances are you don't: the bony orbit,
the tattered leather edges
and soft caps—atonement never ends
with naming what you've done.

Still Your Hand

I keep everything at bay

       don't kill yourself

Being busy means falling

       into each task only so far

Farther sometimes—

       I'm happy when lost

in love or work—still I avoid

       such things   Why avoid

happiness   Nestle with me

       in the safest place (our bed)

Spin down, spin down

       bourbon or TV

I veer into my life and it's here

       where we fail

at lots of daily things

       Will timid-me

decline change

      even freedom   or maybe

I mistake

      abiding love

for mere timidity

      an error that could ruin us

I have a lovely shrink

      but the mind is SO SLOW

You?

Having Been Briefly Held Hostage by Masked Man with Knife

Sunday, in the grocery store,
I wheel my cart toward the back corner,
by the cold cuts and box wine.

Out of nowhere, hyperventilation
launches in my chest. And tears—
ridiculous.

Then Monday comes, and I need coconut
(aiming to be normal, care
for someone *else*),

I drive over, and pulling in,
another blast of sobs—
What's up with the Safewa—

~

After a week, I went to the kind of yoga
they do in the dark, clench and release,
not for exercise but to relax.

Bolstered corpse pose for an hour.
The floor was surely level but I kept
flinching as if to catch myself

from sliding off. Until I saw the raven
and realized that over some long while
I'd fallen pretty far into my mind's recesses.

I had been so good! Right arm, right leg,
and forehead. Left arm and leg . . .
but now I saw my body on a tarmac,

and hopping in the dour way of ravens
came the raven: dream intrusion
in the stubborn body purge. Thought

and Memory were the names
of Old Norse birds. Little pets
to the god of war. My raven

came toward the pie-graph shape
between my legs, splayed open on the concrete,
engine oil stains. *Oh, there you are,* I thought,

still with me. Agile, pearlescent. A messenger?
Of mourning or of luck? The teacher said, "Come on back
to the sound of my voice, feel your hands

against the mat." Which one was it? I wondered:
Thought, i.e. not-knowing, or *Memory,*
reiteration. Why a tarmac?

My body, laid out where it could never be,
amid signals and departures.
The noise there, fat tires of the trucks.

~

How quickly the incident
became a dream rotation: the assailant,
fearful and surefooted in person

(locking the door without leaving fingerprints,
later making his catlike leap
to the balcony wall)

but sleep or pseudo-sleep transformed him
all kinds of ways. Conversion
to acquaintance, threatening at home

(not work). Then other forms: the raven,
the canal, and then himself again:
he wears the black bandanna

he breathed and spoke through,
his wide fingernails and tattooed central fingers,
line drawings in plain black, *Prison tats,*

someone said. The sheepish way
he tucks the knife into his sweatshirt
as he explains his exit plan.

Everyone wants to tell me who approves
(among their friends and confidants)
of what I did and didn't do. Or I sought

approval? There is no way to register
the story, I have learned,
and not evaluate the victim.

I lived, so *Lucky me,*
or I *did well,* or the whole
story's overblown.

I know I've never been so *on,*
alert. Fear came much
much later, as a force I could identify.

Now I go to yoga nidra
every week. A contract with myself,
a duty, to reckon with whatever

needs to surface: secret
compartments in the floorboards,
ravens, or one raven,

picking at junk jewelry on my bed.
In the dream I last remember from before,
my husband hanged himself

just as I was leaving in the car.
I saw his silhouette
in the front door's frosted glass.

I ran back in, too late. Memory
pecks away at Thought,
vice versa too. What happened to that guy?

Did he rape or kill some other person?
After he ran so hard away,
maybe he just slept it off.

Can You Hear My Dog?

Not in Paris, France,
surely. Not in
Sevastopol, Crimea,
woof woof.

He's not what they're
worried about over there.

Little comfort to my neighbors,
I know. But the dogs of war
bark far from here.

Instead, a romp
and wrangle, terrier and spaniel
tool around
the cinder-block perimeter.

Inside, the news is on.

The puppy drowns
it out;
      who knows
if he means to warn

those unseen voices
behind the fence
(he's so ferocious)
or just say hi . . . *I'm here!*

The bombs are for those itsy
bits and pixels on your screen.
Go on, turn it off,

I've got a tennis ball—

Saturation

I.

Did you call the police—

I mean, an ambulance,

says Rakeyia Scott, recording
the cops who shot her husband.
He better live, she says.

She talks to them like any old American,

Oh, there's trouble,
call the police,

but she revises. *I mean.*

~

I'm as white as Reykjavik in winter. I'm some person
in a county with its own cartoon sheriff—
not long ago four officers in four cars
came to reassure my youngest son,
home alone, the sound he'd heard was only wind.

II.

Rakeyia's sheriff said that to release
the squad car dash cam footage
would exacerbate distrust.

How horrific is the video
if withholding isn't worse
than what it shows?

My sheriff doubled down
on how the president is Kenyan.

Her sheriff goes by *Chief.*

Mine is famous for Tent City,
convicts in pink underwear, car-wash raids.
A *posse* of old guys with guns.

We laugh or cringe, we wring our hands, we vote.

"We."

Some of us tremble,
or die in custody, that too. We all know it.

III.

Rakeyia knew in her bones
this solution:
call-the-police,
also she knew:
keep filming.

IV.

In photography, *color saturation*
is the intensity of a color
expressed as the degree
to which it differs from white.

Saturation bombing destroys targets
beyond "necessity."

Saturation coverage distributes
one story everywhere.

We all trust our instincts
as if we were not more sponge
than mind.

~

Henri Cartier-Bresson says
when making photographs he replies
to the *geometry awakened*
by what's offered.

Ted Cruz flexes his menace
by asking if sand
can *glow in the dark.*

The news tells us one thing ad nauseam
until the next erases it.

Resist, Rise up

A man lies dead beside his minivan.

People love sleep, and acquiescence. They complain
about the boot heel but laugh
when it's on someone else's neck—

Each call *Get woke* at risk *Resist*
of being swallowed *Rise up*
by some other open mouth, some other
proof straining in its frame. You have your viewfinder:

you see it, don't you? Crop in,

prove you have an eye.

First Elegy

The night my grief passed through me
most completely,

I was making dinner.
I had lit the grill and reached as ever
to give a quick metallic scrub

and then I realized
you were ash.

It was the day
however many days
after your death they'd said
cremation would take place,
which hadn't struck me
until the puff
of these ashes in their shining chamber

flung at me the knowledge
of your body gone, incinerated, no mistake,
no hope—

       me a zero stuffed with breath.

A swarm of tears, and cries like

none that I had ever made
hauled through me, hauled
my "soul" my presence
of mind my poise my
being-anyone-at-all
into a place of menace, the place

where losing you meant losing everything
about the way I see, make sense.
So I learned what the words mean
in accounts we always blandly read
of ululation, dull eviscerating words, *wracked.*

My husband now my oldest man observed in awe
and the way he knows me also changed.

He was a cleat and I was the boat, roped but
thrashing the rope—

You left me, who made the world seem safe,
who aren't even a bone anymore. Your mottled
mica skin that tore itself in those last days,
how quickly it must have crinkled up and gone.

Who would I show it to?

[Merwin]

I so much trusted your capacity for delight.

Some suicide I've been able to see as an end of deep suffering. Your suffering was not to me invisible but outweighed by your curiosities, your sweet absorptions. Birds, nephews. Dancer pose.

I've tried, but I can't see your death as an extension of seeking.

Come back. I felt this also after my father died. *Come back.* Plea at the base of the diaphragm. Low-down. *Come back.* It frightens me, everything caving toward death's sealed halo. A halo in the gut—

Our last conversation was about my father's body in the hours after he died. Because I got to sit with him. And you described a moth you'd watched fold itself up for death. Am I an idiot? I found you cheerful, as ever your associative pluck and empathy and generosity alive between us.

Man of sorrows. Your white hands, your frail shins. Red hair but softly red, a shell-color.

One night I was cooking alone in the yard, small fire, small steaks. A nighthawk swept into the light between the trees, two sweeps, two lines it cut, and just as my mind flickered toward recognition, sending up your name, —it disappeared into the dark. If that was you, then why did my father send no sign?

Breaker

As you spoke my chest was like the electric panel

on the east-facing cinder-block wall   all the circuit breakers

like little sideways middle fingers

clicking up   You thought I was laughing

but I was having a power experience, dis-

connecting, switch flipped

off

      I told you I was listening hard, and I *was*

listening all right but only partly

to the rundown of faults and crimes

only partly to the pain that drove you and drove you

and that I am the maker of—   I am

I make pain for you and you think it's a goal

therefore a score

                (I am trying

to see   if

    how   or when this is true)

I've spent six seven months

trying to listen to myself, trust my inconclusive

timorous listening and those switches

the ones outside   they prevent overload

short circuit   which means power unimpeded

where power should not even be

click click click click click

the whole box

You said you didn't know "box" was slang for vagina

(what were we looking at?)

That happened yesterday too

Last night my chest closed like a small steel cover

snapped tight in place

Hel-*lo*   is what I felt

I don't know who I said it to

II.

Sieverts and Joules

Maybe there's a new way to be nuclear, not using rods with their troublesome impermanent cladding, their uncoolable fuel, a new way to make less waste and reuse the waste, too, not maybe, this is *in the world*, waiting to be confirmed and approved, *refined*, waiting to be allowed to open up some air.

Maybe then it's okay to love the world. Or to love it and not immediately crumple up in fear. . . .

Sieverts and joules: the sieverts terrify, exist only to measure fatal exposure—8 sieverts mean you will die, sometime between ten minutes and two days from the moment at 8 or above. First, severe vomiting, severe headache, severe fever, incapacitation.

Sieverts and joules: these beautiful words for power, for the creation of motion, for the danger of power, propulsion, to move is to touch, a sievert is a deadly joule—

but maybe we can retool, rethink, make energy more safely? because we want to love the world,

despite the easy-living imposed dormancy.

(Foucault told us; so did first Bush.)

Imposed dormancy in which we buy corn syrup and drive home to some dragons-and-incest TV. While we watch, we hold smaller blue lights in our hands, like nesting Russian dolls of connectivity except those dolls you know eventually the last one is a stone.

I am a teacher. I lather them up about openness and aliveness and not drinking the corn syrup, but also I have spent the last ten years powering down—

I smell this foreign laundry, this other sweater,

the air full of woodsmoke and rain,

the cooling towers in the distance sending out steam in a Cheshire whorl, saying, What about a new way?

You can fear the world or love it, right? If you are free.

If you aren't, you would probably think (if you ever even came to hear it) that this observation was not *a bit obtuse* but lame, oblivious;

still the freest people are so often the most fearful. Too much to lose.

If you believe you have power you have to prove it in love

which I recognize as a principal essential to Christian thought, if not practice, so measure your sieverts and measure the joules and can we please do real things

can we

choose instead of pray

I can't make myself be good but maybe—

Cool It

I'd like to take up running again,
fuck the weird bone pain
where my toes meet each other
and grind into the ground—

pain is part of all good things?
A lesson seared into my forties,
like Didier sears the latitude and longitude
of the forests where they cut the wood for his sculptures
into his magnified (magnificent) seeds. Chestnut seed
made of chestnut, eucalyptus of eucalyptus. At the Opening
I leaned down and touched them,
forgetting the prohibitions of art.

I want to be able to run—
not outrun—but run alongside
the thrum and the pace of the world.

Today, nursing my irritations—for instance,
a book by a colleague, a friend? that uses my name
in this prurient slashery way . . .
Okay: years I've heard these jokes,
still, it's my *name,* is it really
the only good title, rich metaphor,
or maybe this usage is mean?

—and either way: in what Heaney
would call her "image-cellar, dream-bank"
this word, my name, has value
as violent sexy cut with precision,
a pink rubber desecration,

and every time I see it I object
to the fusion and smear. The theft.

So today I wish I could run.

I'm touchy, I'm sad—

I want my lungs to burn that away.

Could I, once and for all?

Instead of flinching at every chipper
re-presentation of _ _ _ _.

I wanted to run.

But no shoes, no proper clothes.

So I walked, fast, and realized
I needed the place with the boats.

And in this (I know) pissy anger
and real sorrow and other queasiness
I beelined for the boats in the trees:

old barges, pulled out of the river
and grown through with reeds.

Ghost boats, rusted, peeling, broken
and beautiful like those pictures
of abandoned Eastern Bloc opera houses,

the boats' mossed-over hatched steel decks full of leaves
(little crumpled fists)
and window shards.

And soft green moss
which if I were sure
no one would see me
I'd touch with my cheek.

I came to the boats
with my woes.

This is the one I can name:

the cover,

and whether or not
I make any mark, any claim.

Whether I want to, who wants
to, and why—

When I think of running,
I think of disappearing:
becoming a slip
of a thing.

And I can see it, my back,
my long legs, the bob
of away and away, down
the darkening road
on the outskirts of town.
I'll go past the barn
where Didier works
filling his seed bank
of outsize unplantable seeds.

In the barn, it's okay
to touch them.
In the gallery, no:
an exhibition
is for looking,
for thinking.

On your mark, get set—

Colony

[Marnay-sur-Seine, France, November 14, 2015]

To be here, outside the city,
to have heard what happened in Paris
after my son in the States
(who texted for proof
I was alive, so silly, I thought,
I'm sleeping . . .)

and then at breakfast Torhild read the news
stiffly into English from a Norwegian website.

—Which was mistaken:
she said the Louvre had been hit,
the Pompidou.

The band that was playing
was Eagles of Death Metal.

On the bench in the dining room
there's a house guitar
with *i* ♥ *metal* painted under the sound hole
in nail polish.

We watch the video of club-goers
climbing out high windows,
a woman hangs by her hands from the third story,
bodies below her
barely out of the door
—they crawled? they were dragged and dropped?

Someone comes and pulls the clinging woman back up and in

so it does not come to pass that she falls
onto whomever covers the ground just below.

People drag more bodies (injured friends? corpses?)
past the ones by the door,
down the alley, away.

What if I had to pull you over the cobblestones
as fast as I could—

Of course, you could watch this in Arizona,
or Trondheim. I'm as safe as the rest
of the surviving world, reading the news,
receiving my own friends' messages of concern.
Some of which move me, I'm grateful,
and some trouble me too: sweetness and prurience,
fellow-feeling, self-insertion . . .

How do we make things our own?

A few Métro stations are closed:
République, Temple.
Those are the ones with resonant names.

The city will close museums, bus lines,
schools, libraries, markets.
But you can still get married
if you make your way to city hall. The killings
will not stop the weddings, nation of love?—

1500 troops

the public told to stay home

Bataclan,
Rue Charonne,
Rue Bichat,
Avenue de la République,
Stade de France,
Rue Beaumarchais

murder or slaughter or mayhem, no language for the lull
while reloading, or reconsideration
of when and where to blow up a bomb
strapped to the chest.

This beater guitar,
acoustic, of course,

now the readiest emblematic *objet*
into which to pour solidarity,
as if I might throw it over my shoulder
(I'm American, like Pete Seeger!—)

and go to the city

and sing.

It's a shock
heart caving in

how fierce is the yes

that would go there to help
or to sing,   make a noise louder than death's noise
than sirens
than cordon tape

surely I'm nothing,
like all the other nothings
who would sing too.

There's a Fuck You in the song

but a particular kind,
open-breasted, empty-handed,
Look how much I can love—

this No proves itself in love

like a wedding
in riven Paris
in November, just two days after Armistice Day.

Last night has no name yet.

I write home from an ocean away,

before there's a name

flush with this circular knowledge:

the only way to say No

comes in a Yes.

Let's sing the Marseillaise with our acoustic guitar
and skip the part about the impure blood,
Allons enfants: let's go, children.

That's what I want to sing:

Let us
be a we
a yes   a *oui*—

a brutal anthem starts a human sound.

Taste and See

Seven very tall French egrets
mill about in a field.
As soon as anyone appears
they take off, headed
as Away as possible.

Their bright gleam in the sky
quickly out of sight—

    Taste and see

Why should it seem holy,
the white glow of their wings?

Conjuring up the language
of my youth in the church:

    Taste and see

    Walk in love

    Go in peace to love and serve

These emissaries, why do I think
they love me even as they flee?

Flight is *proof*
of love?

That's some American female
masochism coming at you
right there.

Or maybe not, maybe just
my own lifted heart
unanswered—it's a danger,
not a balm.

Hold

"Where, where are the tears of the world?"
—Roethke, "The Lost Son"

I.

I am reading this book about human
consumption, how our sense—
and headlong pursuit—of *thriving*
depend, in institutional,
ineradicable ways, on resource
depletion. To the point not yet zero,
the same as zero: everything dies.

My friend has long deftly compared
21st Century America to late Rome, empires
in decline, but this is different,
and larger. Self-destruction

not only of one mode of social living
but of *all life,* all the earthly conditions
that make us possible
as we are. The bees as they are,
the wheat.

To thrive now
means actually to wreck
the future for everyone else.

Both my employer, a university,
and my children's school
(devoted as they both are to the common good,
or commonwealth—)
run "Thrive" campaigns:
do you feel the at-odds missional tension?

To help students,
to advance administrators' careers . . .

Success always defined in terms of surpassing,
preeminence,
because the proof of my value
is *It's better than yours*—

To thrive is to harm, I am reading and learning,
our impulse
to optimize, flourish—is why we will die.

"Buy it"—

Wait, the Midwest was right all these years?
Those leftbehind flownover towns?

II.

Yes, I'll go with the Roman numerals,
thanks.

III.

We could consider analogous forms
of thriving-as-deathgrasp:

like when we set a low goal
so surpassing comes easy

(elementary math standards,
carbon-emissions caps);

or when we value
measurable things
not just *more than*
but *in lieu of*
the im- (or less)
measurable ones,

utility above all
but "utility" defined
down to a competitive pith—

(STEM vs. Humanities
for example; and
growth vs. breath).

Effective corruption
such as rules over us
depends on a bait
and a switch: here is your
traditional marriage,
so you don't notice
your nontraditional
pension.

Pay no attention to—

        —a form of corruption occurs
when the speaker plays
to confirmation bias.

Who's listening, who's supposed
to be listening?

Did you hear: "*the critics,*" like Chekhov's letter to Leontyev?

Or ". . . *the man behind the curtain*"?

Empty barrels rattling in our ears.

IV.

How do we imagine
"resource depletion":
the words go slack,
as dead as the grass.

V.

Skinny polar bear wakes up

two months early;

attics full of dead bats;

robber-baronesque mansions

immersed (like Atlantis,

water swirling through paneless

second-story windows, third-);

more houses shattered by storms,

just a row of brick chimneys,

and that one canted closet sheared

off of the rest of the house

still full of recyclables, aprons on hooks;

empty acre after acre of sand.

Syrian infants

and med students

en route, unsurviving.

Others who drowned in the hold.

Those oxen in Ghana

who graze fields heaped

with motherboards

and seeping chip chemicals:

an occasional fire

licks up from the ground. . . .

Have you seen

the seabird stomach

autopsies?

To look, you'll need the URL.

To look, you'll ignite the systems

of power and, you know,

commit resource

depletion

like one of the

best.

VI.

In fact, if I show you this poem
(by email, a draft,
or later, in a magazine, a
thin little book—),
the poem that cannot save
a bird
will contribute to killing them,
us.

I saw two
great blue herons
yesterday

and all day today
I've wanted to tell you.

VII.

An old insult comes true:
not worth the paper it's

VIII.

The thing is,
so much of the world
stays beautiful.

Convincing.

That fabulous gray wingspan
mirrored in riversheen, flying low
over the water that grooves
between the apparently
endless birches. . . .
Now and then he releases a predatory (or defensive—) cry.

Farmed birches with golden leaves,
geometrically exquisitely aligned.

So many places cancel
our sense of the dire.

Cloister me—

Cloister me forward.

IX.

Look at me:
calling out for protection
i.e., failing to protect—

Abdication the undoing sin
of our time
(*all* time, this time).
How do we stop
being quick to forget?

X.

The joy that comes from the heron,
and awe and gratitude,

they also came when I found that glowing secret
lake of violets
filling an indent of New Hampshire hills,

they come when the ocean
furls and flickers in a pink stripe of dawn,

and they come too when the moon leans forward
over the mountain, huge, like an award
for being in love—

XI.

love too!—these ardors
we take mostly
as reassurance,

proof that all will be well.

My book says doom

is too large an idea, our helplessness too large.

We can't embrace a solution that renounces
the only life we know.

And yes ardor

is a high

we still

get to feel.

You might decide

to find yours,

and breathe it,

and not

tell a soul.

XII.

I don't mean ardor will save us, *ka-ching!*
Only it's better than no ardor,
and better than our other hunger

(to accuse).

Worm, be with me. This is my hard time.

Does the book

mean to say

only art

(art and thought)

can hold sway?

Sway as in solace,

Or solve?

XIII.

Norway takes refugees only on wheels,
not on foot. And kindly Norwegians
may not bring people across in their cars.
You must not walk.
But you can come on a bike.

So the Russian border is heaped with bikes of all sizes:
neighbors who want the migrants gone
bring them to the one side,
then riders abandon them on the other. Safely in.

Cold road,
lined with STELS.

XIV.

This is the world.
And we have to choose
what to do while it's ours—whatever level of doom
you accept or deny.

Swim in the Seine? Okay, east or west
of Nogent and its nuclear plant?
which way the current, the wind. . . .

Those stone steps leading down to the water,

                                        meet me there.

Ways and Means

I.

From Dutch "weg" and German "Weg"
to move or to carry,
and from Old French and from Latin,
intermediary: this is how the first Congress
identified the work of revenue
(getting and spending).

Our intermediaries—taxation
with representation!—
would lift whatever weight
and place it where it might best serve.

They posited a public trust, oaths and vows,

we *cannot* imagine.
I don't mean, They were pure and we aren't.
I mean, There is no uncynical eye
in America watching
these guys (mostly)
and trusting them.
We are a nation
either jaded (trusting none)
or allied (trusting only the likely
venality of the opponent).

II.

Do I trust you?
Turns out there are many territories
in which to answer this question.

Physical danger, and you can intervene,
possibly at great risk to yourself:

yes. I bet you would for me, and
would I for you? I like
to think *yes*.

More pressing: don't we still,
after nearly a decade of reunion,
meet each other with caution—
doesn't caution flare?

I have lived ten years
like a winter tree

and I don't know how
to green up. And you

must have it worse: you
were armored to the chin for years
before I came along like respite (ha—).

The further into the past
the past falls,
the more we seem to have survived it.

Save when *typical*
rushes up from nowhere.

Not nowhere, but a place we always think
we've escaped until we haven't yet.

III.

So if I've spent this time abroad,
and managed to open
my "self," the clenched
musculature of daily competence,

opened and then found
all the loveliness openness provides,
keen perception (light on the rampart,
smell of timber, the questions people ask,
taste of roast chestnut, local champagne—),
and keen surrender (to all
I've avoided or retreated from,
tree schlooped inside its trunk—)

then the question is:
do I share

it with you
or protect it from you?

IV.

Ways and Means: plural:
not one way, one mean.

What language and what currency
can we *use*?

I've felt your sweet willful
marital enthusiasm
surfaced in a fear of losing me

not in joy
of any kind.

I am no (longer a) giver of joy.

 Oh, gifts:

> I should have left
> you a gift,
>
> something to stumble on
> maybe in anger
>
> or in a hurry
> that stops you
>
> and undoes
> a piece of the harm
>
> of today.
> One of our mussel shells
>
> (still tasting like salt),
> a sycamore leaf,
>
> fancy shampoo.
> And I meant to bring
>
> something to sleep in,
> of yours, of you.

I didn't, though, leave or bring any token.

What would we say if we met honestly
under the stars we used to see as blessings,
advisors. There is no

contender. But I am not sure I can contend
with you, us, tenderly, contentedly.

Watch it!

You know how lightning never lasts long enough
to get a good look at it,

and your eyes do this thing,
as if they could grow larger, widen out of your face
trying to see *enough,*
longer, more—

this happens also when the heron passes: too quickly.
Today I lucked into seeing how richly blue
are the tops of his wing-feathers.

Or I think so, I think they were
a kind of luminescent dark cobalt,
but it was over so fast,
could not coalesce into something *I know.*

Come back! I'll be better, I'll *see—*

III.

Soon Scrap Heap

Look at all that pollution over Tempe.
The sky and the freeway one color: cement,
like the fallen wheelbarrow
skidded up against the barrier
of the carpool lane
coated in its own adhesive chalk,
gray cough of commerce,
of "growth." The powder of delayed
but certain obsolescence crusts
its wooden handles, grooved and dry.
Like everything here, dry enough
(cracked, gaunt, reduced
to some dwindling pith—)
not being dust yet
amounts to citizenship,
still votes.

Oh! not everyone old
is dwindling pith! Here
we must depend
on *that*. Retirees,
the monsoons turned into haboobs,
right? You remember,
the creosote smell of the rain,
the glaze—

Can I make the joke about white chickens?

Shall we just keep staring into the rearview mirror,
the barrow upside down . . . oh look, the cops are stopping.

Some Verses

Light vs. Dark

    Lyric vs. Discursive

        Language vs. Disco!

           Lark vs. Dodo—

           There it is:
           song and extinction.
           Bits and zeros
           lay down each warbled track.

Like to the lark at break of day

(First poem I ever had by heart,
thirty years now of my swimming in its DNA,
it swimming in mine—)

From sullen earth sings hymns at heaven's gate

For the record, the lyric isn't just compression
like those running tights, the lyric
loves a thought inside a frame. Arrival,
then containment. A canvas stretched so taut
it pushes light away.

Arising

Look at Senju's two paintings:

vast black-and-whites, one the daunting mountain
with its shadow-copse, a hiking story, the Sublime;

the other an abstraction, X-ray of maybe what a thought looks like,
what distraction looks like spilling its white smoke,
its wet white smoke in rivulets. Smoke falls, it wafts,
it blocks our easy looking toward the dark. We shuffle
up identities in order to stay alive here. The mind's keen
eye goes in, toward the faraway dense dark, but never
fully passes through the veil. What we want, and how we're
separate from that, which makes it possible to want
at all, it all. The veil of *what else, what else*—
                                      "I see you."
That's what this painting says to whoever looks. Not mirror, not
yet: *it* just *sees* me. Or you. And lets us know, *Haply*

I think on thee

The mountain is discursive! It's even a story, each crag
qualifies some detail, adds plot or texture, admits
or claims a point of view. Whereas the X-ray of attention:
that's the lyric utterance, abstract, seducing by usurpment
of my mind (my mind is *mine*, then Senju's, then mine,
    then his—)
and then my state,   for thy sweet love,   such wealth brings

But *we* don't scorn to change our state with kings
                            —not for love and not for money—

in fact we like to disappear, and to "identify."
And art incites such eagerness to relinquish
self,
      goodbye, goodbye, hello, hello,

I'm in disgrace with fortune.

And men's eyes.

I all alone beweep—

And now you see it too. The lyric makes it ours together, fuses us.
Look: the dark, anyone can say it's there;
anyone can point. What frightens us
is all that mediation. All that filtered light.

The song of my pending extinction permits my staying alive.

Stayin' alive.

Ah ah ah ah—

Come Winter

Sometimes I'm not sure whether I want to talk *to*
or *about* the dead—

In the memorial garden, the minister
had already spread the ashes,
as we'd asked. He showed us
where: beneath the ivy
and the pachysandra, easier to look
because of that green filter, that veil.
I'd almost come late, and my heart
raced with rage-at-the-delay
that was really panic-about-the-event.
Your body in the pachysandra—no, your *remains.*
The flagstones, the pine with generous boughs.
Traffic rumbled behind a wall of shrubs.

I wanted never
to stop
thinking toward you.

I decided I did, after all, want to touch
what we'd been given to touch.
I knelt and pressed my hand
into the loosely turned earth and ash.
One hand that would go,
and one that wouldn't, rigid at my side.

The two youngest boys came quickly
to the spot and knelt, like me, and each one
also pressed one hand into the ground.
And looked at me. And squeezed his hand
and brushed it clean as best he could
using only those same fingers, that one hand.

They were eight, cousins, tight.
My son pressed his palm into mine,
and I tried to think of what it meant,
our palms like that, the not-dry
not-familiar clay pressed in between.
To mark each other, or to draw
grief into the flesh, as with a cream.

When he let go, I pressed my own two hands
together—spent the day furtively
pressing palm to collarbone, palm to forehead, cheek.

All day when my son came to see me, checking in,
(in the pew, at the reception)
he always clasped that hand with his.

That's one of the first things you missed.
Along with the look
they gave each other: co-conspirators,
boys who giggled the night before,
standing a nervous distance from the man
(embalmed, tuxedoed, looking
like a groom tipped over on a cake)
whose casket stood waiting, alone in an adjacent room,
for the service after ours.

Stint

In Arizona we have different ghosts
than you have back East.
You might assume I'm being coy—
politics, our love of guns and private prisons
and underfunded schools and Botox
and silicone tucked under the skin
like a little shield to protect our hearts
from—
              What? Losing in the NFL?
The elimination of art and music and PE
and even Wednesday afternoons
from elementary school? But that's not
what I mean. Not skeletons in the closet, no.
If we dig a six-foot hole
we use a jackhammer.
The Earth's crust here is asphalt
and cement, even in "nature,"
cement-like. To plant a rose
you use a jackhammer. To plant a shrub
I need someone (picture him) to bring a jackhammer.
Think of the ghosts.
They have to contend
with our inability to imagine them.
They transition with difficulty
between the surface of the earth
and whatever lies below.
We are prone to ashes, here.
We have claimed to love
the desert scorch and so we burn
in the end, which means
our kids, they less expect
the ghosts of yore. The ghosts we
presumed in the attics of New Jersey, Illinois.

These kids have enough to worry about.
They don't hold their breath
driving by each Memorial Garden.
You'll have to really work
to haunt us here.

Can You Hear My Dog?

If so, my apologies.

He's bouncy, he's talking to the mutt
next door about interest rates
and gun control
and diabee-bees

—he knows most Americans
are less bouncy than he is,
he's worried for our arteries,

63% of you are obese,
he says, loudly, over the fence,

to women with jog bras
and strollers with mud flaps,
but he can't see them,

doesn't know how hard
they are already working.

The fence is tall cinder blocks
so he can't know

what Lucky even looks like,
Lucky to the north,
and the digger next door,
whose name we don't know,
to the west, yappity yap.

Plate 79   Crocodile   Valley of the Kings, Egypt

Dear Keats, why Italy?
You'd have loved this crocodile, ancient
bas-relief, smiling with his eyes closed, one plunge
from the meaty neck of a gazelle.
O happy crocodile, O John,
he looked like this for centuries
before you lived and died, blissed out,
savoring his knowledge
before savoring his meat.
He looked like this when Linda took
the photograph, in 1989.
And now, too: in Egypt, in how many photographs
(of hers, of others') reprinted in how many books,
and here, this poem, the scent of dinner
in his nostrils as he smiles,
a happy happy happy happy croc,
a wakeful, sturdy, unwarnable gazelle,
who doesn't know,
perpetually, his doom, though he's smiling too:
a gloater? Stone gazelle.

The Collar

Is this a metaphor:

two dogs playing

one spaniel, one terrier

the game involves

one dog sliding

the other's collar off

but tonight

in the dark yard

the dogs squeal

panic-rage of mortal

animal combat

(Mr. Point-and-Flush

vs.

the Thrasher of Rats, is there also

a bobcat?) Neighbors call

over the fence *Do you*

need help? But I don't know

yet, can only

see a blur, hear

a growl, pair of growls

Then I register

the blood

so much blood, and shrieks

and wheezes, and two rufous

bubbles distend out of

Cosmo's nostrils

golf ball–sized

I throw a table on its side

because how else distract

them from each other

Cosmo looks at me

and blood flares

His eyes—

My eyes squint against death

and I reach in

thinking to unclamp

the other jaw

locked at his throat

that must be the cause

(now the stanch?)

but I can't, my thumb

at the mandible hinge:

why won't it unclench?

They both

seem to know unclamping

isn't happening, lady

We are three bodies all

touching the axle but what

holds this wheel

together   just rat-killing terrier

compulsion? If I let go

the animals will turn animal

again and one or both

will succeed in no one's quest

Good dogs

I was sure the collar-game

had already been played

but find leather which must

be the axle

and using two

hands now I trace

toward the buckle, tighten

in order to release

and—off—

they are free

of each other   Those hooked

canines had twisted into the collar

unloosably, now finally undone—

We all tremble and noodle

our heads together

and I check everywhere

for holes in dogs

Cosmo still sneezing

blood onto the bricks

onto my (when did they come)

neighbors   onto my jeans and arms

There are two small

but spurting lacerations

at his muzzle so

he breathes in blood

which then comes back out

again as golf balls

All the blood on the rat-thrasher

(plentiful, striping

his beard, his brindly face)

belongs to Cosmo

Such small

lacerations

all this mess

The bad dog humbles

himself head down

Cosmo chasm-looks

at me opening some portal

to another field of being

who knows what

he means

       I know

this look is all

he has to give and he wants

me to have it so I

do not look away

Already he only bleeds a smidge

He sighs the sigh

of survivors whose

lungs require

other muscles   other air

No puncture

of that throat

it inflates and subsides

like any breathing

sleeve, frisson

of normal . . .

The terrier wonders

about playing again?

Cosmo turns his tender

nose toward not-that-dog,

shoulders him

out of the way, sighs wearily

The collar says COSMO

and our coordinates

sole purpose safety

but it tangled, throttled

him   He stands and breathes

—the whole sky on offer

not blasted, not wasted—

Connie and Tom

leapt over a cinder-block

wall to help me

That's no metaphor

Those are my friends

Pop Goes the World

We drove to Tucson in the cuspy light
of a morning moon—
caraway seed, eyelash,
lemon zest over mountains we knew
were there but couldn't see.

My daughter sang
all through both hours of the drive.
She played her favorite songs
and belted out the beltables,
and as we neared the city,
the sun showed us which pocket
of the sky it had been tucked
inside: it said, *Light starts here,*
the deep southeast, the idea
of Mexico. In G.

She sang. The one about the farmhouse
and the girlfriend who broke it off too soon,
the one about the anorectic
whose father was an asshole,
and one about a founding father
cheating on his wife.

She's made of both the lyrics and the chords;
who is she? Where are her friends?
She holds music in her
throat the way my friend Martina laughs,
the love of laughter flooding in
along with thought, the observation
and the joy of making it
equally potent, and here in the car,
the joy of just how sad the song knows
she is sometimes, often actually.

Lost One, Kept One

I lived a couple decades
in one doomscape:
worrying love would fail
to sustain us, worrying
beloveds would die
of breathlessness or self-
release. Now I know
the world will soon
refuse us all. I think with panic
of my children's children,
or their children, or will my own
even bother? I hope
not. Let the line
end with us. Because
I doubt we've got fifty
years before the suffering
converts even relatively genial
humans into cutthroats
and the books and movies
I can't bear to read
or watch come true
and having saved money
won't matter, having read
anything won't matter,
having recycled, having
xeriscaped, having closed the tap
while brushing, packed lunches,
used thermoses not
Styrofoam, having
felt guilty about plastic
bags, having returned
most bags to the grocery-store bin,
having sent shoes

to Angola, having spoken
sometimes and remained silent
too among perpetrators
of market egregiousness,
having owned stock,
held on for the long game,
having taught Oppen,
Neidecker and her mops, Berryman
and his juniors and lonesome
outcries, and having loved
now and then the wrong
people (Suzanne, I owe you
an apology—) and having said
to the other moms
This is a *parenting strategy,*
letting small children
wander and fight and fall,
This is the cultivation as they bled
or annoyed more attentive parents
of independence, having planted
a weak purple jacaranda
that just wouldn't grow
but nonetheless held on,
having pulled over to help
the cat who then died
in the car and let go, of course,
brand-new soiled station wagon,
having put my hands
into the earth where my father
was ash turned in with the soil,
rhododendrons, pink cherry blossoms—
having donated to save the bay
but sometimes used cleansers

with detrimental pHs,
having grown old enough
to want sun like a honeysuckle,
despite cancer and spotting,
sun, *in a good way?*
Having sat weeping
over articles on the death
of the oceans, sailors
on routes poisoned
by everything, who see garbage
infinities, who see no fishes,
who blame spills or overfishing
or warming or all of the above.
Having minimized
additives, having installed
or acceded to Lo-Flo
showerheads, bought organic,
declined Walmart, McDonalds,
for years, having appalled
some and disappointed others
(too far left, too mainstream)
having made pals in long voter lines,
marched on Washington,
signed petitions, written my congressmen—
everything futile? Everything
outright doomed.
What do I do if still
I am moved. Not
optimistic, not fooled,
even by my own desire
to be fooled, to be hopeful—
those years of false drama
turn out not to have been false:

one of them died
and one didn't, and here we are.
Having lost one, having kept one.
To have and to hold.
Having will kill us,
all the too-manys.
So: hold.
Hold me back
from the brink of recognition.
This the only footing
in hope, only
stay.

"Near-Eternal Material"

accrues on the beach.

The paper says *in staggering amounts*

and shows a photo of Indonesian coast

not made of sand but washed-in plastics,

so many colors—a *pretty* photo, for a second.

I never had (nor wished to have) a diamond

but I had a ring. Naked finger now.

"Near-eternal material": it's like the chorus

of my life: what to object to, what to strive for.

One feels nourished in the ocean, floating. Or

by my mother's house that's true:

her nearest beach seems clean,

endlessly clean, not full of syringes,

not full of indissoluble soda or bleach bottles,

just gleaming sand, gleaming beige and blue . . .

You'll see the occasional tampon applicator

or bubble wand or six-pack yoke

but mostly the water's edge seems compellingly okay.

Love was meant to temper us into near-eternal material.

This photo shows a mile of trash.

How to understand *eternal*

in a world both beautiful and wrecked—

(depending on where you stand,

depending on how you look).

A nearness we couldn't endure;

a material— *not* trash, not everything's

a symbol or synecdoche, even when

the chorus makes you want to sing along.

It's a gamble, seeing likeness everywhere,

looking for what sticks.

Inertia, or harm, or by-the-grace-of-god

good luck. The beaches need some stewardship;

the oceans, the landfills, need attention.

Whereas the smaller *we*, our effortful

attentions: let's let them travel elsewhere.

Let's look hard at something else.

Notes

The epigraph is my translation of part of "Pêche lunaire," by Greta Knutson, from *Lunaires* (Paris: Éditions Flammarion, 1985).

"Furious Deities," "What to Do with Dead Birds," and "*Plate 79 Crocodile   Valley of the Kings, Egypt*" are written in response to photographs by Linda Connor, collected in *Odyssey* (Chronicle Books, 2008).

"Having Been Briefly Held Hostage by Masked Man with Knife" takes its definition of thought from Adam Zagajewski's essay on the painter Czapski, "Toil and Flame," in *A Defense of Ardor* (Farrar, Straus and Giroux, 2005).

"Saturation" quotes Henri Cartier-Bresson's *The Mind's Eye* (Aperture, 2005).

"Sieverts and Joules": the italicized phrase in the last line comes from Jason Isbell and the 400 Unit's self-titled album (Lightning Rod Records, 2009).

The book described in "Hold" is Roy Scranton's *Learning to Die in the Anthropocene: Reflections on the End of a Civilization* (City Lights, 2015).

"Some Verses" describes two paintings by Hiroshi Senju: *Day Falls/Night Falls* and *Cliff.*

Acknowledgments

I am grateful to the editors of the following magazines where many of these poems first appeared: *American Poetry Review, The Awl, Bennington Review, Boston Review Forum 3, The Collagist, Colorado Review, Connotation Press: An Online Artifact, Ecotone, Harvard Review Online, The Laurel Review, The Literary Review, Ocean State Review, On the Seawall, Ploughshares, Plume, San Diego Reader, Scoundrel Time, Southern Humanities Review, Tin House,* and *Zócalo.*

"Temple Example" was reprinted on Poetry Daily and on Poets. org. "First Elegy" was also reprinted on Poetry Daily.

Working with Jan Vičar on the images for the artist's book of "Hold" made the poem better, and Jan's prints are one of the lucky amazements of my life.

~

My love and thanks to the early readers of these poems: Martha Rhodes, Chris Nealon, Kevin Prufer, Eric Pankey, Camille Guthrie, Mark Halliday, and Ted McNally.

Also, for help translating "Hold": mille remerciements à Mathilde Rousseau Domec, Sylvain Gallais, Laurence Mills, et Laétitia Brion.

~

For fellowships and solitudes that supported work on this book, I'm grateful to the CAMAC Centre d'Art in Marnay-sur-Seine, France; the James Merrill House in Stonington, Connecticut; and—at Arizona State University—the Department of English, the Institute for Humanities Research, and the Virginia G. Piper Center for Creative Writing.

Thanks to Peter Covino, Michelle Caraccia, Sarah Kruse, Mary Giaimo, and everyone at Barrow Street Press.

Love and gratitude to Ellen Bryant Voigt, Lynn and Jeff Callahan, Oscar and Celia McNally, Jean Ball and Jen King, Alix Ohlin, Emilia Price, Jen Bredin, and Cyndi Cross (*& all*—).

Sally Ball is the author of *Wreck Me* and *Annus Mirabilis*, both from Barrow Street. She is an associate director of Four Way Books and an associate professor of English at Arizona State University. She lives in Phoenix.

BARROW STREET POETRY

Hold Sway
Sally Ball (2019)

Green Target
Tina Barr (2018)

Adorable Airport
Jacqueline Lyons (2018)

Luminous Debris: New & Selected Legerdemain
Timothy Liu (2018)

We Walk into the Sea: New and Selected Poems
Claudia Keelan (2018)

Whiskey, X-ray, Yankee
Dara-Lyn Shrager (2018)

For the Fire from the Straw
Heidi Lynn Nilsson (2017)

Alma Almanac
Sarah Ann Winn (2017)

A Dangling House
Maeve Kinkead (2017)

Noon until Night
Richard Hoffman (2017)

Kingdom Come Radio Show
Joni Wallace (2016)

In Which I Play the Run Away
Rochelle Hurt (2016)

The Dear Remote Nearness of You
Danielle Legros Georges (2016)

Detainee
Miguel Murphy (2016)

Our Emotions Get Carried Away Beyond Us
Danielle Cadena Deulen (2015)

Radioland
Lesley Wheeler (2015)

Tributary
Kevin McLellan (2015)

Horse Medicine
Doug Anderson (2015)

This Version of Earth
Soraya Shalforoosh (2014)

Unions
Alfred Corn (2014)

O, Heart
Claudia Keelan (2014)

Last Psalm at Sea Level
Meg Day (2014)

Vestigial
Page Hill Starzinger (2013)

You Have to Laugh: New + Selected Poems
Mairéad Byrne (2013)

Wreck Me
Sally Ball (2013)

Blight, Blight, Blight, Ray of Hope
Frank Montesonti (2012)

Self-evident
Scott Hightower (2012)

Emblem
Richard Hoffman (2011)

Mechanical Fireflies
Doug Ramspeck (2011)

Warranty in Zulu
Matthew Gavin Frank (2010)

Heterotopia
Lesley Wheeler (2010)

This Noisy Egg
Nicole Walker (2010)

Black Leapt In
Chris Forhan (2009)

Boy with Flowers
Ely Shipley (2008)

Gold Star Road
Richard Hoffman (2007)